TREES

WEEPING WILLOW TREES

John F. Prevost
ABDO & Daughters

Published by Abdo & Daughters, 4940 Viking Drive, Suite 622, Edina, Minnesota 55435.

Copyright © 1996 by Abdo Consulting Group, Inc., Pentagon Tower, P.O. Box 36036, Minneapolis, Minnesota 55435 USA. International copyrights reserved in all countries. No part of this book may be reproduced in any form without written permission from the publisher.

Printed in the United States.

Cover Photo credits: Peter Arnold, Inc.
Interior Photo credits: Peter Arnold, Inc.

Edited by Bob Italia

Library of Congress Cataloging-in-Publication Data

Prevost, John F.
    Weeping Willow Trees / John F. Prevost.
      p. cm. -- (Trees)
    Includes index.
    Summary: Provides basic information about the weeping willow tree, including the structure of the plant, its economic uses, and the pests and diseases that affect it.
      ISBN 1-56239-619-6
    1. Weeping Willow--Juvenile literature. [1. Weeping Willow.] I. Title. II. Series: Prevost, John F. Trees.
    QK495.S16P75 1996
    583'.981--dc20

96-6061
CIP
AC

ABOUT THE AUTHOR
John Prevost is a marine biologist and diver who has been active in conservation and education issues for the past 18 years. Currently he is living inland and remains actively involved in freshwater and marine husbandry, conservation and education projects.

Contents

Weeping Willow Trees and Family

Weeping willows may grow to be over 70 feet (21 meters) tall. They have long, drooping branches that often touch the ground.

Willow trees have leaves that fall off in autumn. Weeping willows are easily grown from **cuttings**. They are fast-growing trees and are easily **transplanted**.

Weeping willows first grew in China. Today, there are over 160 kinds of willows in the world. Many of them are small bushes.

In North America, there are over 100 kinds of willows. They are used as **shelterbelts**, shade trees, and in wildlife plantings.

Weeping willows are known for their long, drooping branches.

Roots, Soil, and Water

Willow trees pull water out of the ground with their roots. Minerals and other **nutrients** are found in the ground water. These are the food for the tree. Without enough food, the willow will not grow or produce seeds. The roots also keep the tree from falling over.

Weeping willows grow well when planted in wet soil. Even if they are planted in dry soil, their large root system will find the ground water. But the roots sometimes plug up sewer pipes in their search for water. Weeping willows should not be planted within 50 feet (15 meters) of any sewer or drain lines.

Opposite page: Weeping willows need minerals and nutrients to grow and stay healthy.

Stems, Leaves, and Sunlight

Sunlight is important to every green plant. Trees use sunlight to change water, **nutrients**, and air into food and **oxygen**. This process is called **photosynthesis**.

The trunk of the willow supports the branches, stems, and leaves and connects the roots to the leaves. This allows water and nutrients to reach the leaves where food is made. The food then travels back to the roots.

The branches and stems of weeping willows are long, drooping, and **brittle**. The leaves are 3 to 6 inches (8 to 15 cm) long, and 1/2 inch (1 cm) wide.

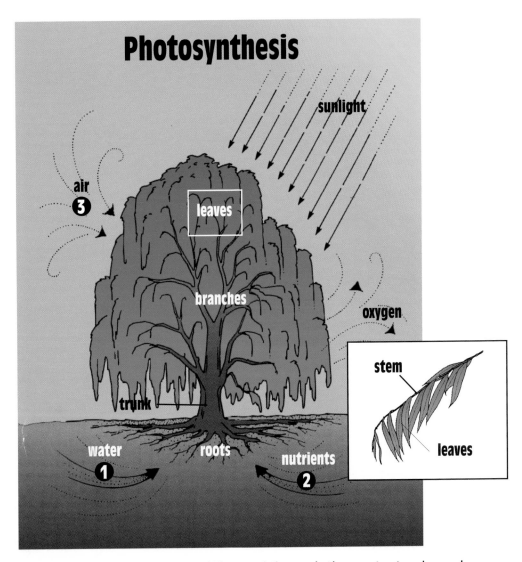

Ground water (1) and nutrients (2) travel through the roots, trunk, and branches and into the leaves where air (3) is drawn in. Then the tree uses sunlight to change these three elements into food and oxygen.

9

Flowers and Seeds

Weeping willows flower in the early spring, before the leaves appear. These flowers are called **catkins**. Male and female catkins grow on different trees. Male catkins make **pollen** that **fertilizes** the female catkins. The female catkins grow fruit.

The fruit on female weeping willows are small, round, and hard. Inside are tiny dark brown seeds. When the seeds ripen, they fall to the ground and sprout new willow trees.

male catkin

female catkin

fruit

*Opposite page:
The flower of a weeping willow is a catkin. They bloom in early spring.*

Insects and Other Friends

Weeping willows are home to hundreds of insects, most of which help the tree. Many are **pollinators** or **predators** that eat **pests**. Birds and small **mammals** such as squirrels, chipmunks, and bats nest in weeping willows and feed their young on pests. Other animals use the tree for shelter.

Squirrels and other mammals nest in willow trees.

Opposite page: Insects make their home within weeping willows.

Pests and Diseases

Weeping willows are home to several insect **pests** like **aphids, borers**, caterpillars, Japanese beetles, and **scale** insects. **Predatory** insects, like wasps or ladybugs, help control these pests.

Diseases also attack willow trees. A healthy tree will resist these diseases. A weak tree may need **chemical** sprays to survive.

Ladybugs and other predatory insects eat insect pests.

Diseases may attack willow trees.

Varieties

There are many weeping willow **varieties**. Most are grown for their different **traits.** Others are grown for their beautiful yellow leaves.

Some varieties do better in hot or cold climates. Some are more weeping or droopy.

Opposite page: Weeping willows are grown for their shade and beautiful leaves.

Uses

Many weeping willows are grown for their beauty. Others are grown to control **erosion** along stream banks and on steep hillsides.

Several types of willows are grown for their long, **flexible** branches which are used to make baskets and furniture.

Willow leaves and twigs provide food for many **mammals**. Deer, moose, beaver, and elk feed on willow trees.

Opposite Page: Weeping willows are often found along streams where the ground is moist.

Weeping Willow Trees and the Plant Kingdom

The plant kingdom is divided into several groups, including flowering plants, fungi, plants with bare seeds, and ferns.

 Flowering plants grow flowers to make seeds. These seeds often grow inside protective ovaries or fruit.

 Fungi are plants without leaves, flowers, or green coloring, and cannot make their own food. They include mushrooms, molds, and yeast.

 Plants with bare seeds (such as evergreens, conifers) do not grow flowers. Their seeds grow unprotected, often on the scale of a cone.

 Ferns are plants with roots, stems, and leaves. They do not grow flowers or seeds.

There are two groups of flowering plants: monocots (MAH-no-cots) and dicots (DIE-cots). Monocots have seedlings with one leaf. Dicots have seedlings with two leaves.

The willow and poplar family is one type of dicot. All willow trees—including weeping willows—are part of the willow and poplar family.

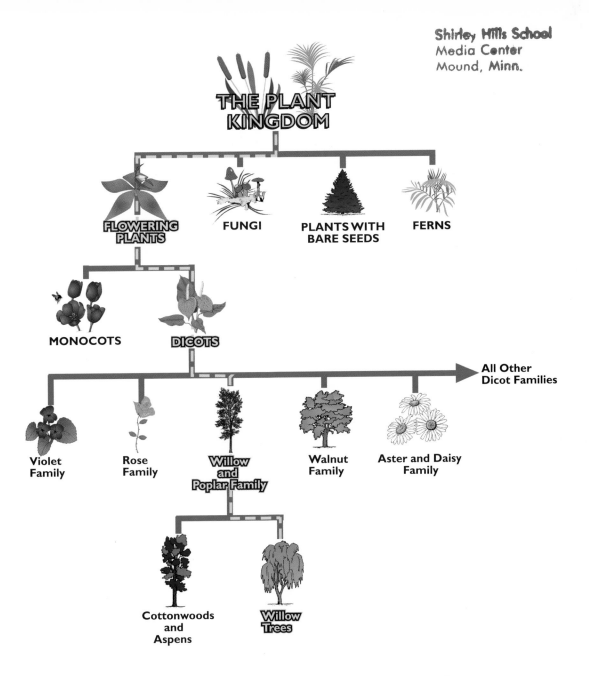

THE PLANT KINGDOM

FLOWERING PLANTS

FUNGI

PLANTS WITH BARE SEEDS

FERNS

MONOCOTS

DICOTS

All Other Dicot Families

Violet Family

Rose Family

Willow and Poplar Family

Walnut Family

Aster and Daisy Family

Cottonwoods and Aspens

Willow Trees

Glossary

aphid (AY-fid) - A small insect that sucks the sap from plant leaves and stems.

borer (BOAR-er) - An insect that digs into plants.

brittle (BRIH-tull) - Easily broken, cracked, or snapped.

catkin (CAT-kin) - The cluster of flowers found on birches, oaks and willows.

chemical (KEM-ih-kull) - A substance used to create a reaction or process.

cutting - A stem, bud or leaf that is used to start a new plant.

deciduous (duh-SID-yoo-us) - Trees which lose their leaves in the fall.

disease (diz-EEZ) - A sickness.

erosion (ear-OH-zun) - The loss of soil to wind and/or rain.

fertilize (FUR-tuh-lies) - To develop the ovule into a seed.

flexible (FLEX-uh-bull) - Able to bend without breaking.

mammal (MAM-ull) - A class of animals, including humans, that have hair and feed their young milk.

nutrient (NOO-tree-ent) - A substance that promotes growth or good health.

oxygen (OX-ih-jen) - A gas without color, taste, or odor found in air and water.

pests - Harmful or destructive insects.

photosynthesis (foe-toe-SIN-thuh-sis) - Producing food using sunlight as the source of energy.

pollen (PAH-len) - A yellow powder made by the stamen that fertilizes flowers.

pollinate (PAH-lih-nate) - To move pollen from flower to flower, allowing them to develop seeds.

pollinator (PAH-lih-nay-tor) - An animal or insect that helps pollinate a plant.

predator (PRED-uh-tore) - An animal that eats other animals.

scale - A tiny insect that sucks the juices of plants.

shelterbelt - A group of trees protecting buildings or fields from wind and other weather.

shoot - A young branch, stem, or twig.

stamen (STAY-men) - The male flower part (the flower part that makes pollen).

trait - A feature; characteristic.

transplant - To plant again in a different place.

varieties (vuh-RYE-uh-tees) - Different types of plants that are closely related.

Index